HOPSCOTCH FAIRY TALES

Dick Whittington

Retold by Anne Walter
Illustrated by Roger Fereday

W
FRANKLIN WATTS
LONDON•SYDNEY

First published in 2009 by
Franklin Watts
338 Euston Road
London
NW1 3BH

Franklin Watts Australia
Level 17/207 Kent Street
Sydney
NSW 2000

A CIP catalogue record for this book is available
from the British Library.

ISBN 978 0 7496 8542 3 (hbk)
ISBN 978 0 7496 8548 5 (pbk)

Series Editor: Melanie Palmer
Series Advisor: Dr Barrie Wade
Series Designer: Peter Scoulding

Printed in China

Franklin Watts is a division of
Hachette Children's Books,
an Hachette UK company
www.hachette.co.uk

Once there lived a poor boy called
Dick Whittington. He had no
parents and was often hungry.

Every week, Dick saw the wagon go to London. He'd heard that London had streets paved with gold. "I'll make my fortune there," he thought.

4

London

5

One day, the wagon driver stopped. "Would you like a ride to London, boy?" he called.

"Yes please!" shouted Dick, and he jumped up on the wagon.

When Dick arrived, the streets
of London looked dirty. "Perhaps
I will find the streets of gold
tomorrow," he thought.

Next morning, Dick still couldn't
see any gold. He begged for food,
but everybody ignored him.

By evening, Dick was weak with hunger. He lay down outside a merchant's house to sleep.

An angry cook woke Dick up.
"Go away you dirty boy!"
she yelled.

Just then, the merchant came home
and saw Dick. "I'm Mr Fitzwarren.
And who are you?" he asked.

Dick was too weak to reply.

Mr Fitzwarren carried Dick inside

and told the cook to bring some food.

Mr Fitzwarren offered Dick a job in the kitchen and a room to stay in. Dick was delighted, although his room was full of rats.

Mr Fitzwarren's daughter, Alice, made friends with Dick. She gave him a cat to chase the rats away.

Dick worked hard in the kitchen,
but the cook still hated him.

Then, one day, Mr Fitzwarren told
all his servants, "My ship sails
tomorrow with goods to sell and
I hope to make my fortune.

If you give me some things, I can
sell them for you, too. Maybe you
will also make your fortunes."

Everybody except Dick gave
Mr Fitzwarren something to sell.
"I don't have anything," he said.

"You could sell your cat," said Alice. Dick was sad to lose his cat but he let Mr Fitzwarren take her.

In the next few months, Dick tried hard to please the cook. But she beat Dick with her pots and pans.

One morning, he ran away.

Dick had not gone far when he heard church bells ringing. "Turn again Whittington, Lord Mayor of London!" they seemed to say.

Dick turned back. He got home just as Mr Fitzwarren returned. "Here is your money from the things I sold," Mr Fitzwarren told the servants.

"And, Dick, all this gold is yours! A king bought your cat to chase the rats from his palace."

"I've made my fortune!" Dick cheered. He shared his fortune out with everyone.

Dick never forgot the kind
Mr Fitzwarren and, years later,
Dick married Alice.

He also became Lord Mayor of London, just as the bells had seemed to tell him.

Put these pictures in the correct order.

Which event do you think is most important?

Now try writing the story in your own words!

Puzzle 2

Choose the correct speech bubbles for each character. Can you think of any others? Turn over to find the answers.

Answers

Puzzle 1

The correct order is: 1e, 2b, 3a, 4f, 5d, 6c.

Puzzle 2

Dick: 3, 6

The cook: 1, 4

Mr Fitzwarren: 2, 5

Look out for more Hopscotch Fairy Tales:

The Emperor's New Clothes
ISBN 978 0 7496 7421 2

Cinderella
ISBN 978 0 7496 7417 5

Jack and the Beanstalk
ISBN 978 0 7496 7422 9

The Pied Piper of Hamelin
ISBN 978 0 7496 7419 9

Snow White
ISBN 978 0 7496 7418 2

The Three Billy Goats Gruff
ISBN 978 0 7496 7420 5

Hansel and Gretel
ISBN 978 0 7496 7904 0

Little Red Riding Hood
ISBN 978 0 7496 7907 1

Rapunzel
ISBN 978 0 7496 7906 4

Rumpelstiltskin
ISBN 978 0 7496 7908 8

The Three Little Pigs
ISBN 978 0 7496 7905 7

Goldilocks and the Three Bears
ISBN 978 0 7496 7903 3

For more Hopscotch books go to: www.franklinwatts.co.uk